Just Be With Bizzy Bee!

Hilary Hawkes

'A clever, simply-written story, perfect to help a child to relax. A RED RIBBON WINNER and highly recommended.' The Wishing Shelf Book Awards

Hello from Story Therapy®
We're a small, not-for-profit/part-voluntary project and member of Social Enterprise UK. Our resources aim to support children's emotional health and mental wellbeing. Our products are available to all, and we also donate annual nurturing gift packs to chosen beneficiary groups.
www.storytherapyresources.co.uk

Just Be with Bizzy Bee

Words © Hilary Hawkes

Front cover image: Teguh Mujiono/Shutterstock.com and MatthewCole/Shutterstock.com according to license agreements

Interior Illustrations and back cover: Pixabay.com Except for bee on flower: Teguh Mujiono/Shutterstock.com used under license, rainbow picture: Bellenixe/shutterstock.com, interior garden scene: image used under license: MatthewCole/Shutterstock.com and Bee puzzles:Tiplyashina Evgeniya/Shutterstock.com used under license agreements.

First edition by Strawberry Jam Books for Story Therapy® 2016, updated 2017, 2018

All rights reserved. No part of this publication may be reproduced, stored in a retrieval system, or transmitted in any form or by any means, electronic, mechanical, photocopying, recording or otherwise without the prior written permission of Strawberry Jam Books. Hilary Hawkes has asserted her rights under the Copyright, Designs and Patents Act of 1988 to be identified as the author of this work.

British Library Cataloguing in Publication Data

A CIP catalogue record for this book is available from the British Library

   Story Therapy®

Abingdon-On-Thames, UK

www.hilaryhawkes.co.uk/strawberyjambooks   www.storytherapyresources.co.uk

Print version: ISBN: 978-1-910257-20-3
Digital version: ISBN: 978-1-910257-21-0

Disclaimer: This book is not intended as medical or professional advice for ongoing or specific anxiety/disorders, and parents, carers etc should always seek appropriate professional help for children in such cases.

A Note for Grown-ups

This book introduces a simple way to teach children an easy to understand method to pause, relax, and become calm and peaceful at any time - in a busy day, at the end of the day, or at times when they might feel anxious, worried, angry or upset. Bees are busy, hard-workers, but at times they simply stop and find somewhere safe to be still and quiet! Just Be with Bizzy Bee helps children recognise that people need to do the same at times. Learning how to relax and just be can help all children calm down, become more focused, manage different emotions or sleep more easily. A relaxation technique/meditation that can be used with children at home or in groups is included at the back of the book.

There are ten tiny Bizzy Bees like this *to find in the pictures of the story!*

Thank you to the following people for their help and suggestions in composing the relaxation exercise at the end of the story: Jill Cofsky (MA Ed) and her First Grade class at A. M. Chaffee Elementary School, Oxford, Massachusetts; Cat Michaels (MS Special Ed and author), and Andrea Harrn (MA psychotherapist and author of The Mood Cards).

It's Bizzy Bee!

He sets off from the bee hive every day looking for flowers. Bees LOVE flowers!

How do bees make honey?

Bees collect nectar from flowers and store it in their 'honey' stomachs. Here it gets turned into honey!

They fly back to their bee hives or nests and put the honey into honeycombs (like pockets) in the hive.

When the honeycombs are full they fan their wings over them and this makes a wax cover over the honey.

"Hi there!" says Bizzy Bee.
"There's lots to do today!
Nectar to be gathered.
I must be on my way!"

Can you help Bizzy's friend through the maze to the flowers?

Bizzy has found some blue flowers.

"Buzz, buzz, buzz!" says Bizzy, as he collects lots of nectar from the blue flowers.

"Buzz, buzz, buzz! These look good!
There's really lots to do!
I'll start right here today,
I really love the blue!"

Next he finds a pink flower.

"Buzz, buzz, buzz!" says Bizzy, collecting lots of nectar from the pink flower.

On he flies. Buzz, buzz, buzz!

And now he's found the pink.

Where to next for Bizzy?

It's hard work, don't you think?

Now Bizzy has found some BRIGHT red flowers too!

Red so bright, orange too.

He works so hard you see.

He hums his buzzy song,

A happy little bee.

"Buzz, buzz, buzz!" says Bizzy and all the other bees.

Bizzy and his bee friends spend all day flying from flower to flower.

They take the nectar back to the hive and then set out again to find more nectar.

Can you spot ten differences between these two pictures?

(See the next page for the answers)

Once honey tums are full
Back to the hive bees fly.
Off again! More to do!
Buzz, buzz across the sky!

Bizzy begins to feel tired from all the flying and all the buzzing.
It's time to stop!
He finds a quiet place and settles down in the warm sun! Bizzy might be a busy bee, but he knows how important it is, sometimes, to stop and…JUST BE!

"Time to stop!" says Bizzy.
"Such busy days for me.
Sometimes I really must
Take time to simply be!"

Bizzy knows the best way to just be!

First he finds somewhere quiet and safe.

He stretches out and relaxes.

Sometimes he shuts his eyes.

He breathes deeply and slowly.

Can you just be with Bizzy?

Pretend you are a bee like Bizzy!

Bizzy finds a quiet place
And stretches out to rest.
He knows a little pause
Will help him be his best.

Bizzy notices the sounds around him, but stays peaceful.

He might look out at the other bees, or the flowers, or up at the sky. He stays peaceful.

He feels the warm sun

and the gentle breeze.

And he stays still and relaxed.

The warm sun shines, and then
A gentle breeze blows by.
As Bizzy rests his wings
He breathes a happy sigh.

Bizzy doesn't move. He doesn't do anything.

He just lets everything go on around him.

In his quiet place he can stop and just be and just breathe.

He waits quietly.

Bizzy feels calm and peaceful and content.

Feel calm and peaceful and content just like Bizzy.

Imagine you're somewhere warm and safe and peaceful…

"It's good to stop a while!"
Says Bizzy. "Be like me!
Sometimes just take the time
To stop and then JUST BE!"

Bizzy stays in his quiet place to just be as long as he wants.

After a while he feels ready to carry on being a busy bee.

Then he stretches again, flutters his little wings and begins to take

off.

Bizzy knows he can stop again and find a quiet place to just be whenever he needs.

You can do the same!

Whenever you need to be still and calm for a few moments, stop and JUST BE like Bizzy!

A Guided Relaxation Activity for Children

> *Directions for grown-ups:*
>
> *You could put on some calming music that your child likes to do this relaxation together or to talk your child through it.*
>
> *Find a safe and comfortable place to sit or lie down away from distractions and noise. You could dim the lights or close the blinds a little.*
>
> *If your child uses a "focus object" consider adding that to the relaxation exercise.*
>
> *Speak in a soft and gentle voice/tone.*

Script:

You are going to be quiet and still – like you are just before you go to sleep.

Take a minute to let your body go still and relaxed from your head to your toes.

Notice if any part of your body is tensed up and not relaxed – tighten up that part (maybe your hands or knees) just a teeny-tiny bit and then relax it again.

Your body is now completely relaxed and peaceful.

If you want to, close your eyes.

Breathe calmly and gently and notice how your breath goes in and out, in and out, all on its own.

Put one hand on your tummy and notice how your body moves when you breathe.

In and out, in and out – slowly and gently.

Now you can take an extra deep breath and then slowly let the breath out like this:

Deep breath in. *(Pause)*. Deep breath out. *(Pause)*. Deep breath in. *(Pause)*. Deep breath out. *(Pause)*.

Now just breathe gently and normally.

Notice the thoughts going through your mind. Imagine each thought is like a white fluffy cloud moving across the sky. Just watch it. What thought comes along next? Imagine the thoughts just floating along.

Take in another big breath and this time, when you let the big breath out, pretend you are blowing air at the thought cloud. Imagine the thought cloud being gently moved across the sky by the air from your breath.

If there is another thought, let that float away, like the clouds in the sky.

Stay still and peaceful for a few more minutes or for as long as you can. Think about Bizzy Bee in the story: safe and snug on the flower. Just Be like Bizzy for a little while longer.

When you're ready, slowly stretch your arms and legs. Wriggle your fingers and toes. Open your eyes if you had them shut.

If you were lying down then slowly sit up. You are feeling more peaceful and calm. Let this gentle feeling stay with you throughout the day. Imagine yourself being happy and relaxed in everything you do today.

Also in the Story Therapy® Series, helping children deal with feelings and emotions:

The Forever Tree

Little Acorn and the Great Big Happy Hug

Stories for Feelings

Stories for Feelings: The illustrated Edition

Imagine! interactive stories with musical backgrounds cd or audio download

For more details and games see www.storytherapyresources.co.uk

www.ingramcontent.com/pod-product-compliance
Lightning Source LLC
Chambersburg PA
CBHW042033100526
44587CB00029B/4397